The Shaman in the Library

Jon Wesick

Acknowledgements

Some of the pieces in this book have appeared or will appear in *Art and Zen Today, Asinine Poetry, Atlanta Review, Backstreet Quarterly Review, BEAT-itude: National Beat Poetry Festival 10-Year Anthology, Black Book Press, Buddhist Poetry Review, Caliban Online, Cherry Blossom Review, Dali's Love Child, Diaphanous, Earthbound Review, Eskimo Pie, Fur-Lined Ghettos, Gutter Eloquence, How Higher Education Feels: Commentaries on Poems that Illuminate the Experiences of Learning and Teaching, In Between Hangovers, League of Laboring Poets, Limestone Circle, Litbreak, Madness Muse Press, Magee Park Anthology, Magpies: A Zoem Anthology, Mannequin Envy, Misfit Magazine, Napalm and Novocain, New Verse News, Nomad's Choir, North Cascades Buddhist Priory Newsletter, Oddball Magazine, Open Door Poetry Magazine, Parody, Poesia, Poetry Superhighway 23rd nual Yom HaShoah (Holocaust Remembrance Day) Poetry Issue, Riggwelter, San Diego Poetry Annual, San Diego Writers Monthly, Scryptic, Sheila Na Gig Online, Spirit First, Still Crazy, Sunken Lines, Synchronized Chaos, Synesthesia, Three Treasures Zen Community Newsletter, Tidepools, Vortex of the Macabre, Waymark, Windmills, With Lyre and Bow, Writers Resist, "The Germ, Sacred Journey, Lothlorien Poetry Journal."*

Published by Human Error Publishing
Paul Richmond
www.humanerrorpublishing.com
paul@humanerrorpublishing.com

Copyright © 2022
by
Human Error Publishing & Jon Wesick

ISBN: 978-1-948521-14-7

Jaguar Image by Charles J. Sharp, Jaguar (Panthera onca palustris) male Three Brothers River.JPG

Content

The Shaman in the Library

Naked except for a loin cloth,
ritual scars, and streaks of red clay
he attends the staff meeting.
Bowl haircut, back straight, face impassive.

Why is he here? No one knows.
Since the library opened he's pushed
the loaded book cart and replaced
Suzanne Somers and Gwyneth Paltrow
in the diet and exercise section.
Trembling patrons pay late fees promptly
when he stands by the circulation desk.

A few parents complain their teenagers
shadow him chasing rumors
of hallucinogenic Ayahuasca vines
hidden in the botany section.
And after the singed carpet incident
management forbade cooking fires.
No more fresh rabbit meat
only packets of microwaved cassava.

He pricks his fingertip at shift's end
and fills out his timesheet with human blood.
It's a good life. His employer provides
health insurance and a retirement plan but

when the wild parrots come
to strip fruit from nearby trees,
he remembers the land of his birth,
his vision quest, fasting to the point of death,
and how his spirit animal came to him.
He remembers inhabiting the jaguar's body,
its savage strength, and the power he gained,
power to take life and heal.
Free from culture and convention,
he hunted at night – the heart-pounding chase,
the taste of wild boar's blood
8

Lorca's Tomb

This pen is a firing squad,
boots kicking in the door at midnight,
black hood over the head, rifle butt to the kidney,
and unmarked grave in a gully.

Who among us dares nick their veins
for ink or peel skin from arms
for parchment? Not me, though

once I spotted Death at a Leucadia café.
Off duty, he regaled admirers
with tales of his exploits – dodging artillery
and machine gun fire in the Ardennes forest,
scaling a tower in 15th-Century Barcelona
to take a cloistered maiden.
We shared a common sensibility.

I wanted to introduce myself
and give him copies of my poems
but I love waking to the sound of the radio
and savoring coffee on my living room couch
so I stole away to write only of paisley shirts
and the safety of hummingbirds

The Writers' Prayer

O Lord, protect Your servants, the truth-tellers.
As we stand outnumbered by malicious armies of dogma and
denial,
       shield us from their hateful blood-soaked weapons
       of cover up, distortion, and reprisal.
Keep us safe from the weight of government repression,
       from fatwahs, inquisitions, censors of the left
       and of the right.
Shield us from attacks by ineffectual parents,
       politicians looking for an inflammatory issue,
       and criminals seeking to shift the blame.
Shelter the purity of expression from commerce's pollution.
Safeguard us from the corporate publishing steamroller
       with its warranties and indemnities clauses.
Guard us from predatory lawyers and burdensome lawsuits.
Guide our works with insight; may we avoid misunderstanding.
Most importantly, preserve our hearts from cynicism,
       lest we, who hold the mirror for others,
       fail to view our own reflections. Amen.

Twenty-Five Definitions of a Poem

Words
  from a mute's lips
A unicorn
  in a Prussian helmet
The testimony
  of a murdered man
Drumsticks
  tapping empty space
Cymbals
  crashing at the end of a line
An orange
    flaming in a young boy's hand

Antelope footprints
    on Diamond Mountain
The granite knees
  of a great nation
Black Stetson
  on a white surfboard
and orca
  his dorsal cutting glasslike water

Beowulf's broadsword, Ned Kelly's iron mask
Steel stirrups
  on a gynecologist's table
Rebel yell, Politburo communiqué
The broken zipper
  on your lover's jeans
Wine
  from an empty bottle
Dimples
  on a woman's hips
Stinking cups of genocide
  black and overflowing
A symphony
  in a bed of snapdragons
Rumi's column, Kabir's loom
The silence

at the end of OM
Memoir
    of a childhood you never had

At the Local Book Display

She was the kind of woman I'd always wanted,
her ample volume on display in the glass case.
I imagined my hardcover next to hers
on Barnes & Noble's shelves,
her colorful dust-jacket wrapped around me.
I wanted to caress her perfect-bound spine,
slip my fingers between her pages.

"Which one's yours?" she asked.
I pointed to a homemade poetry pamphlet,
twenty-five Xeroxed pages held together by staples.
My dreams of the New York Times Bestseller list went limp.

"Don't worry. It happens to lots of guys," she said,
"What you gotta do is go to a bookstore,
find out what everybody else is writing,
and write the same thing.
Chicken Soup books are really hot now."

I saw what my life with her would be like.
Each day I'd join the faceless drones
at Mediocrity Corporation
and toil to pay for a tract home that looks like all the others.
I wandered to the buffet table and took a cube
of Swiss cheese speared on a toothpick.
When no one was looking,
I slipped out the door
and ran.

Addicted to Drama

Long ago, perhaps even before birth,
a hack writer installed his Juan Corona
in my middle ear. The typewriter's clacking keys fill
gaps in my knowledge and crowd out understanding.
He casts me as a romantic lead. The dirty blonde
sitting across my breakfast table wears an expression
sour as grapefruit juice. Her plaid robe's careless fold opens
to a roadmap of varicose veins on lumpy thighs.
I stare out the window through gaps
in the fence's white wooden slats
and hope to glimpse the woman meant for me –
the right one, the nude sunbather whose breasts float
like Nuryev's grand jeté.

During my drive to work, Congressman
Lavrenti Beria squawks on the radio news.
I recognize coded orders from his cabal
of crypto fascists to their brainwashed zombie hoards.
A villain in a tan Ford Bronco reveals himself
by lumbering into my lane. I become an action hero.
The script calls for a fight in a parking lot.
After escalating insults and provocations
I'm supposed to bury his head in the asphalt
with a slick Steven Segal iriminage.

But I'm too late for work. I sneak in the back door
as my boss' shaved head and high-collared cape
recede around the corner. If he'd caught me, the Evil Sargon
would have banished me to planet Telcom's underground mines,
where I'd scrape plutonium from rock walls with bleeding fingers
while choking on thorium dust. Until the revolution
I can only further Sargon's maniacal plans for world domination.
I limit the damage by leaving before 5:00.
The hack has entertained me for so long that I mistake
his voice for my own. Desperate to end my oppression
I see force as the only option.

At the Farmhouse that Inspired Anne of Green Gables
(Cavendish, Prince Edward Island Canada)

I can almost see her, strands of red hair over pale breasts,
warm Browning automatic and empty gin bottle on her
dresser while the strict schoolmarm's body cools in the
drawing room.
Life would never return to normal
even after blistering those pretty hands
digging a six-foot hole in the garden.
The sound of automatic weapons fire
            from the guerillas in the hills
                    grew closer by the day
and that briefcase of rum runner's cash
could not buy the constable's silence.

So she fled to Paris
survived by lowering her panties under the Pont Neuf
the few francs paid by sweaty workmen
enough for a glassine envelope of Turkish heroin.
Part of the Lost Generation she slept with rats and fleas
until Gertrude Stein taught her the pleasure of a woman's
tongue.

Then to Spainand a doomed affair with Lorca
She joined the Abraham Lincoln Brigade
was captured by Franco's forces
When the interrogating officer
shoved his thick fingers under her skirt
he found the hidden hand grenade
its pin removed seconds before

Bukowski's House

Even in death
he guards his privacy
his ghost
cussing out fans and would be gawkers
so I send my imagination
infiltrating the San Pedro city limits
prowling where he lived

The one-story house of brick and wood
front window a Cyclops eye
peering unconcerned
while the outside world goes on its foolish way,
chain link fence, no garage
only a weathered BMW parked
one wheel off the driveway
on dying grass

I enter
not for the alcohol-fueled rages
nor for the screaming women breaking glass
but for the 4:00 AM solitude
notebooks to fill,
Brahms on the radio

Waking at noon,
plastic-upholstered chair at the kitchen table,
tattered bathrobe and walk to the mailbox,
the safety of a warm Southern California breeze,
no place
more important than here

Thirty-Two Flavors of Rejection

Some days are hard as glass
and not as clear. Days
when the knuckles of confidence
bloody themselves against granite doors
and the only bandage is a flimsy
cellophane of denial. Days
when equations take up torches and pitchforks
and the electronics is nothing but a box
of flashing lights and baffling parts.

When the odds are long
and the rewards meager,
When the bed is empty
and my date has a double chin,
When the novels don't sell
and ten years of college is not enough,
When the economy serves
the bitter melon of rejection,
I reach for a pepper shaker
of resentment.

So many years now,
I've gotten used to the flavor.
My successes are not sweet. They taste
of crowded airports, lonely hotel rooms,
and the blandness of routine.
Even if a pastry falls from the winners' table,
my tongue detects a chemical aftertaste.
I step away from the banquet
and return to my self-imposed diet

A World Without Flowers

In the crusty-eyed hours of morning
we search each other's' bodies for answers.
I ask her breasts about refuge
while she interrogates my lust
about belonging and how
to make love stay.

We find no answers
in the tangle of sweaty sheets
and salty taste of skin
yet I'm compelled to ask
again and again.

Hormones fade
and leave me with amnesia.
Who is this woman? Does her womb
scheme against me? Even an arm
over my shoulder would provide a clue
but I can't ask lest I reveal my weakness.
So, I do what I do best
play along
    stall for time
        pretend

A Postindustrial Romance

*...we live in a society that is both competitive and in which we
are incessantly evaluated (school, university, performance as
writer, poet or businessman or sportsman). The only place
where you hope to stop that evaluation is in love.*
                                                    Eva Illouz

Donna married my paycheck
on an unseasonably warm autumn day.
Bridesmaids in antebellum gowns fanned themselves
and congratulated her on her good catch.
I still have the postcard she sent
from their honeymoon in New Zealand.

I wanted them to be happy.
Even when pricing helium futures
at the zeppelin factory,
I'd set down my slide rule
and imagine her moaning with pleasure,
my paycheck between her thighs.

When the downsizing began,
she sat at my paycheck's bedside
holding its hand telling it not to give up.
At the funeral pallbearers had to restrain her.
In her grief she began to live for her job
staying at the office long after dark
and subsisting on frozen dinners.

To console her I explained that in today's economy
love depends on the trade balance with China
as well as myriad decisions by executives
in large corporations. Now she's dating again.
If you're interested, forward your resume
along with a copy of your tax return.

Or Perish

Solving one integral stands between you and a satisfied life.
You'll be a professor in a cashmere sweater,
have an intelligent, capable woman on your arm,
and drive an antique sports car because genius
is a license to be eccentric. How wonderful
when the best minds pause to hear your thoughts
and wide-eyed students say you make science fascinating!

You open a thick book of integral tables,
search hundreds of pages, and find only the sinking feeling
that your future townhouse with its pre-Columbian artifacts,
season tickets to the theater,
and vacations in the South of France
are getting more and more unlikely.

You change variables but each x transformed to u
becomes another low-paid, temporary post-doc.
You move to more desolate cities leaving friends behind
to work on increasingly mind-numbing, desperate projects.
Your lover abandons you. Aching for a human touch
you sleep alone in a noisy, one-bedroom apartment.

Your hand cramps after filling pages with letters, symbols,
and eraser smudges. When you try integrating by parts,
it becomes clear that after years of high-tech serfdom
you'll have only these useless pages. An Internet search
traps you in the quicksand of mathematical irrelevance.
You curse the teachers who encouraged you.
The tension in your shoulders could snap a steel cable.

Your future written in pencil –
a future of frayed sweatshirts, cheap shoes, bill collectors,
a subterranean credit score, and tasteless beer in rundown bars

Brother, can you spare a Lagrangian?

Hilbert spaces, basis vectors, inner products, the
Hamiltonian, symmetry, conservation laws, rotation matrices,
bosons,fermions, the Pauli exclusion principle

Although your background is impressive,
your qualifications don't fit our needs.

Momentum space, Fourier transforms, Dirac delta function,
c-numbers, creation and annihilation operators, commuta-
tors, Feynman diagrams, unemployment insurance

Did you look for work during the week of November 17?

Time dilation, Lorentz transformation, Klein Gordon equa-
tion, scalar, vector, pseudovector, liquid drop model, quan-
tum rotator, magic numbers, island of stability

Your qualifications don't fit our needs.

F=ma, action reaction, second order partial differential
equation, infinite series, integration by parts, saddle points,
calculus in 3-D, the work energy theorem, Gauss, Ampere,
Faraday, Maxwell, Mathematical shortcuts are the best! V, I,
R, C, jωL

Congress expands the number of H1B visas to compensate
for the "lack" of American scientists and engineers.

Silicon surface barrier detector, sodium iodide crystal,
photomultiplier tube, o-ring, scattering chamber, amplifier,
preamplifier, logic gate, coaxial cable, analog to digital con-
vertor, thesis defense.
"Congratulations, Dr. Wesick!"

Your qualifications don't fit our needs.

They said education was the key to my dreams
And so I followed the mob
BS in physics then Ph.D.
Now I can't find a job

They told me I was building my dream
Of a fascinating career ahead
Then why should I have to struggle so
Just to earn enough bread?

Once I studied quantum. It was fun
The math symmetric in time
Now out of college my career is done
Brother, can you spare a dime?

Ivory tower's packed full to the sun
Corporate needs don't align
My career was over before it begun
Brother, can you spare a dime?

Fake It 'Til...

Dad taught me that insecticide
paved the road to success.
Raised on stories of lives free
of gnats and roaches, I thought
that was all it took.

Then an angry pustule
sprouted from Dad's forehead.
"Is it a bot fly?" I asked. "The one
that lays its eggs in living flesh?"
"Never say that!" Mom's slap
spun my head.

We hid father in the garage
until the larvae hatched
and his body crumbled.
Mom swept him into a dustpan
and left his remains in a Hefty bag
at the curb. We never spoke
of him again.

Decades later, termite mounds
of platitudes replace missing men.
A Ford Mustang waits patiently
for a transmission that will never come.
Cicadas scream where once weekend jazz
played from Peterson's garage.
Jimmy Hackford teaches himself
to catch a ball

Ode to a Porn Star

In a world of concrete and shame
only you, my vessel of desire,
demonstrate intimacy.
Despite slurs and scorn, you remain
comfortable in your body,
comfortable that others have bodies.

Humble as the Pope washing feet,
you kneel for our pleasure. One minute
your body is a roof that shelters the timid.
The next, a banshee emerges
from the fire between your thighs.

Hair stringy, skin slick with semen and sweat,
you summon strength to part lips again and again.
Echoing the sound of the universe's birth,
your moans shake the heavens
tumbling gods from their thrones
to walk with humans and demons alike.

Mars Needs Actresses!

There again on an old movie
on late-night TV, those familiar blue eyes
and spattering of freckles across her nose!
Karen Allen, whatever happened to her?
And where did Ellen Burstyn go?
Did Roseanna Arquette vanish from her Beverly Hills home
leaving "Croatan" carved on a tree trunk?
After starring in all those DH Lawrence adaptations
did Glenda Jackson jump in a time machine
and travel to Mexico with Ambrose Bierce
or simply join Neal Cassady for a walk in the desert?

I miss Debra Winger's funny nose and crooked eyes
as well as Margot Kidder, Molly Ringwald,
Penelope Anne Miller, and Adrienne Barbeau.
Maybe they're cruising the Bermuda Triangle
on the Mary Celeste or sunning on a tropical beach
with Jimmy Hoffa. Maybe they took part
in a secret, government project
at the Philadelphia Naval Shipyard or hijacked a plane
and parachuted over Washington state with the ransom.

When discussing why aging actresses disappear,
the simplest explanation is best.
UFOs! Alien abductions!
Mars needs actresses!

Another Love Poem (That Didn't Work)

Come, Love
be the antacid
that soothes my burning heart
and lie with me
on pumpkin spice
strewn over my truck-bed liner.

Your feet are dainty
as hybrid subcompacts.
Each leg, slender as a 3.5-inch
nitrous-ready driveshaft
with chromoly yoke
and solid-body u-joints.
Your navel, a glazed donut.
Your breasts, round and firm
as the tennis balls
my Labrador never tires of chasing.

Your neck, graceful
as a Swedish floor lamp.
Your gaze, hypnotic
as the smartphone ap
that summons our rideshare
to paradise.

I want to drink sweet Moscato
from your cochineal lips
then sober myself
in the dark-roast Americano
of your hair.

My passion is a 2.9% APR
credit card, its chip and PIN
unlocking the bounty
of your desire

The Having Corner

There's a corner of her bed
where everything is safe

There's a corner of her bed
where he can hang
onto
his opinions

whether strong

or

just a flake

of snow

melting on his tongue

The Buddha in My Bedroom

Donna pokes her head into my house and speaks
the word of everyday life. She offers this freely
like a shampoo bottle in a friend's shower.
Touch, once unobtainable, now immediate and solid.
Arms nestle my head to a reassuring shoulder.
Her skin emits the almost imperceptible odor of home.
Muscles that screamed to be held grow quiet.
She frees breasts from her bra, takes my hand,
and leads me into the bedroom,

where the lips of the green bronze Buddha
on my home altar appear to move.
"Seeking enlightenment while having relations
is like cooking rocks in a rice pot."
"Did you hear something?" I ask.
Donna shakes her head and unzips my slacks
with the practical dexterity of a mother undressing her child.
Before we set sail in the ship of affection with its paper hull,
I imagine many unhappy rebirths, ten thousand lifetimes
reliving Miss Hawk's high-school algebra class.
"Maybe we should turn the statue toward the wall," I say.
Donna pulls me to her. "This too is Buddha."

Meditation Instruction

Even if an A-frame of chicken bones
is all that's left of your last meal
and the executioner will come for you soon,
settle your awareness in the here and now.

Even if the turkey is still raw
ten minutes before the banquet,
Even if you lost the winning lottery ticket
and your future prosperity tumbles with pants in the dryer,
practice the here and now.

Even if your joke about the porn star
brought a grimace to the pastor's lips,
Even if a fart loud as an air horn
erupted at Toastmasters,
let waves of awareness return you to the here and now.

Even if your neighbor uses your lawn as his dog's toilet,
Even if that SUV takes two parking spaces,
Even if you obsess over your upcoming scene in Tarantino's
film, Even if your Nobel Prize acceptance speech is tomorrow,
let your mind be a redwood rooted in the here and now.

Even if a naked Angelina Jolie (or Brad Pitt)
calls you from the bedroom,
Even if a new Lamborghini gleams in the driveway
and the keys are in your pocket,
let your mind be an immovable mountain
in the here and now.

Even if you fantasize this immovable mind
will make you an action hero,
Even though this poem is only a metaphor
and such a mind is impossible,
Even though Einstein proved that now does not exist,
your here and now are enough.

Ode to the Sesshin Participants

Scientists of consciousness
holders of postgraduate degrees in awareness.
The meditation hall is your laboratory.
Knees and backs aching, feet numb as clubs
you gather wearing sweatpants and *rakusu*
to hear the endless repetition of a *Boz Scaggs* song
in your thoughts while certain that damn *jikido*
should have rung the bell ten minutes ago.

Yesterdays' breakfast clogs your bowels and you would kill
for a half hour without someone knocking
on the bathroom door.
You hope to finally get six hour's sleep.
And although discovering
buckwheat *zafu* make great pillows,
you toss and turn all night,
wake at 5 AM, and do it all over again – sit, walk, chant,
move *zabutons*, obsess about when to brush your teeth,
and unfold *oryoki* napkins made into red warning flags
by first-day tomato sauce. Despite wanting to punch
that guy blocking the coffee pot, you make *gassho*
and bow anyway.

Worst day of your lives. You don't belong here,
don't belong anywhere so you pack your bags
and are out the door when you decide to give it one more day.
Sometime before breakfast a geyser of joy erupts inside.
Smells of delight waft from the kitchen,
One with fruit trees and rocks you sit in the garden at ease,
convinced you are the Buddha's children.

Somewhere past joy your inner narrators finally shut up
leaving your minds still ponds.
You who couldn't wait to leave
now find kindness in the rules and schedule.
And when you return to the world outside
you find it noisy, strange, and cruel

Ode to Laziness

Stillness
is a bowl of gold-flecked porcelain,
endlessly fascinating.
Authority's voice pours in gray dishwater
overflowing the rim
and soaking life
with anxiety or boredom.
Empty it!

Sometimes the best *zazen*
is in the easy chair.
Supported by an inner tube, I float
in the present moment, limbs limp,
chin resting on inflated plastic. Even here
duty's voice whispers the myth of productivity.
"Swim laps. Win a medal
at someone else's pointless game."

Practice idleness wholeheartedly instead!
Resting in the exquisite stillness
like a stone with senses
is to sit atop Laozi's ox.
Then the doves will return to the concrete pond
and the rabbit's tail flash in the grass

Another Zen Poem

In awe of the mountain, disgusted by the toilet.
Buddha is far away.
Bowing to the toilet, bowing to the mountain
(still slightly in awe).
Hung-jen presents a robe and bowl before dawn.

Holding Buddha close.
The world becomes a toilet with no mountains to be seen.
Bodhidharma leaves town, saying he's heading out west.
This windbreaker's full of holes, and the Tupperware's stained.

Bowing to the world (still slightly disgusted).
A tattered jacket hangs in my closet,
while the microwave warms lunch in a plastic container.
Nothing else to do now but
        bow to JC Penney
           and Tupperware,
              bow to silk
                  and Tang dynasty
                  porcelain.

Reading Zen on the Train

It's in these pages – the isolated monastery
gnarled plum tree blossoming in the snow
bell at 4:00 AM, old monks, black robes
zafu, zabuton, full lotus
sound of a wooden block in the courtyard

>Cell phone ring
>"Hey Bro, I'm on the train by Solana Beach!
>Where's the nearest liquor store?"
>Neither tattooed hand covers the mouth
>that coughs infectious spores into shared air.

Bell reverberating into silence
sore knees, lonely candle
Even here, the dust and dirt of this world
Do you want something more than this?

>"My supervisor sets me up for failure.
>Those guys in Irvine haven't cooperated at all.
>When I went to her for help, she said
>I should develop a working relationship with them.
>Working relationship."

Drum beat, *kesas* on shaved heads
"I wear the *Tathagata's* teaching saving all sentient beings."
Hanya Hara Shin Gyo
bows, a cascade of bells

>"Tickets please!" The conductor
>carries his silver punch from seat to seat.
>A boy with Down Syndrome recites the schedule.

Breakfast – a ballet of chopsticks and lacquer bowls
work, kitchen
wash rice, chop vegetables
a sutra in a bag of mushrooms

The Coaster approaches Del Mar.
Passengers scan the ocean for fins.
A baby dolphin jumps from the waves.

The abbot, an ancient buddha
the koan – polishing a brick to make a mirror
No ultimate – No Buddha
No everyday – No teaching
Fish cannot live in sterile water.

Seattle Zen Poem

Sometimes I sit and watch my thoughts
come and go like clouds in the sky.
When one stays too long,
others gather,
and soon there is a shower.
It rains a lot here,
but last night it was clear,
and I observed the moon and the stars.

The Ticket

I left my emotions at the dry cleaners, because
my laundry hamper
just isn't a safe haven for my heart.
Months later I found the claim check
buried under financial records
and rediscovered vibrant colored garments long forgotten.

Now
my limbs pulse with life. Plum trees
bloom in the snow. Their falling petals
clothe the world in freedom. I see the universe
with fresh eyes, open
the throttle flat out, no
obstacles ahead, proudly
display my purple threads,

but the stale smell of sweat
compels my return to the anonymity of wash
and wear cottons,
my Greater Self hidden
for months or years at the dry cleaners, until
I find the ticket
once again.

The ticket,
next time -
a ticket to far Tibet,
where I hear they wear scarlet robes every day.

December 31 –
a Meditation on Impermanence

During the day, I pay bills,
dust, and vacuum
to greet the future
unencumbered.
Then to the meditation hall.

Stillness whiff of incense,
the anonymity of darkness
A lone candle paints the Buddha statue gold.
Mind obsesses as usual.
Plans, worries, a craving for black forest cake.
Maybe, just maybe
    the internal narrator will hush.

Outside
    shouts of joy fireworks
The year turns.
Sadness tinges the celebration.
as the rocket of mortality launches me into old age.
Fools threaten democracy. Progress is only a slogan.
The temple bell sounds.
    Chanting
I want my old year back

Three Pounds of Flax Seed
(a reply to Philip Levine's "Philosophy Lesson")

What is the Buddha?
Three pounds of flax seed - Tozan
The oak tree in the garden - Joshu

Robe stained with sweat
Zen master Tozan toils in the store room.
I take a burlap sack from his hands,
ponder how mass warps clocks
and meter sticks.

Philip Levine stirs cream
into his coffee as a waitress sets
a plate on the Formica table.
I sample the omelet but find no answer
to his eggs-istential dilemma on my fork.

Why is the work of the hand glorified
and that of the mind disdained?
Why was the monk hauling books
throughout China scorned?

Tear old Joshu's oak tree from the soil
and turn it roots facing the sky.
Discuss Gödel's Incompleteness Theorem
with the gardener and Karl Popper with the grocer.
Check in hand the waitress asks if I'd like anything else.
"Yes, I'd like to know how closed, timelike loops
affect causality."

What is the Buddha?
A Feynman path integral
The Cauchy Schwarz inequality

After Twenty-Two Years of Zazen

Smoke rises from a stick of pine incense.
Distance hushes children's voices. A songbird symphony
rides the stillness that smoothes the ocean
to perception's limit,
but a razorblade lurks in the rice cake.

Squawking charges of old abuse
and baseball bat revenge fantasies
a raven of hatred flies from my forehead.
In a crowded warehouse store
momentum carries my shopping cart
into the heel of a woman blocking the aisle.
She turns with a dirty look.

Behind me in the checkout line
the Dalai Lama shakes his head.
Images of bayoneted monks flicker on his retinas.
I turn. Brown eyes hooded by epicanthic folds
ask a question. The answer
floats beyond my grasp like a helium balloon
unattended for a millisecond too long.

Buoyed by dense air the balloon rises
through the heavens of form and no form
to arrive at the infinite sea of milk,
where Vishnu floats dreaming the dream that is the world.
With each snore a billion suns arise
and wink out of existence. Yet the balloon waits.
The slumbering god snorts, scratches his nose,
and turns on his side.

In the House of the Eternal Now

Faith and doubt
shelve books in the library.

Famine and gluttony plunk down plates
on the blond wood table.

Lust wrestles nude with celibacy
on starched white sheets in the master bedroom.

At dawn the landlord lights incandescent bulbs
saturating the living room with darkness.

At midnight saints and murderers
hold hands in the brilliance.

Touching this instant
a wind from before the universe began
breathes life into stones, rivers, paperclips,
and the coffee cup on the desk.
In this place beyond time the dead arise.
Their limbs glow with radiant pink flesh.

The Poppies of Treblinka

drink sunshine like the pale, naked skin
of daughters huddled hands over breasts and thighs.
Fire-red petals flicker in a breeze that supports
the screams of husbands and sons, first in the showers.
Daisies and cornflowers too bloom beside rusty barbed wire,
the path to death runny with the loose stools of the terrified.

Trains of stinking, crowded cattle cars come and go
unobstructed by the ten thousand grasses. Galaxies
wheel through the vast cosmos, unconcerned
with the necklace of teardrops, each reflecting the others.
A man with pliers yanks gold from dead mouths. We've yet
to extract screams that can cross light years of empty space.

Summer clouds roil into a giant Buddha preaching
the perfection of this instant. Is that thunder
or rifle shots I hear? The birds of thought
leave no trace in the sky, but what of the stupa
of black, oily smoke rising from burning flesh?
Tell me, can this meditation cushion
survive the crematorium fire?
If not, how can I set it anywhere?

Everybody Loves a Hanging

City fathers and their adoring wives,
smells of kettle corn and grilled sausage,
Mrs. Wheeler's social studies class,
Chamber of Commerce, the mayor in top hat,
the sheriff gun belt and brass buttons gleaming,
rattle of rollercoaster wheels
and screams from the tilt-a-whirl.

Children underfoot, weaving
through the crowd to get a better view
or tugging mothers' sleeves to point at steel tubs
where men with tattooed arms twirl
wisps of sky blue cotton candy.
"See Miss Trixie, the woman with three breasts!"
barkers yell. "Sorry kids, this one's adults only."

After the main event – fireworks!
Maybe a souvenir to help you remember –
T-shirts, postcards, a 1/24-scale replica of the gallows.
Photographers are standing by
to take your picture with the bloodstained rope!

At the Corner of Midnight Crisis and Broken Dream Boulevard

I am not my job today.
Yet this business becomes my life,
consuming my final precious hours.
Corporations rape me
then demand I smile,
while they button their trousers.

The sun set on youth and opportunity hours ago.
Night came hard and fast
giving no warning.
I find no shelter,
so I remain trapped on this boulevard
laid bare to the pimps and whores
who ogle me with dollar bill eyes.

My muscles strain to move through viscous air
thick as maple syrup with heat and humidity.
The local tough wears a sleeveless shirt.
It reveals weightlifter arms –
arms that threaten to crush me,
if I don't pay eleven dollars rent
for standing on his corner.
I hand over a twenty
and wonder how I'll survive tomorrow
on nine dollars change.

I lean against a brick wall,
that tears my shirt
and scrapes tender skin from my back.
Scam artists congregate
drawn by the smell of blood.

Dreams flicker fainter and further apart
like violet light from the burnt-out fluorescent bulb.
I hear its buzz
and the sound of glass breaking far away.
A guy in the alley sings something in Spanish.
It is 11:59 PM.

A Coffee Shop on the Coast Highway

Yoga schools and surf shops pass my window
on the 7:45 southbound train.
My last comfort,
the old yellow wooden coffeehouse,
fades farther
and farther from view.
The smell of biscotti baking,
nose rings on the counter girls,
their pear breasts under soft sleeveless
shirts that reveal tattooed shoulders
all left behind
for a scarred linoleum floor
and soul-killing brown cubicle walls.

I sit with lockjaw in the morning meeting,
while a petty tyrant humiliates his lackeys.
My phone rings with impossible deadlines.
Venture capitalists scream through middle managers,
frightened men, for returns on investments.

Earth rolls into afternoon.
I dream of reading Chandler & Bukowski
on the veranda by the gnarled pine tree,
while birds brave the wooden owl's glare
and hop from table to table in search of crumbs.
The memory of jasmine tea
cannot moisten my dusty throat.

At day's end I'm further behind
than when I started.
I glimpse the coffee shop
from the 6:05 north bound's window.
The girls have swept the floor
& put away the dishes.
They locked the doors a half-hour ago.

Unwanted Guests

lodge upstairs
and turn my apartment into a slum.
In front of open blinds
Greed fornicates with a different woman each night.
After one brings him to orgasm he discards her
like one of the used condoms he tosses in the bushes.

Lassitude roasts pork ribs in August.
Vitality drips from my open pores in the heat,
until I'm too weak to rise from the couch
and change my sweat-stained shirt.

Disillusion pours alum in the well.
I drink the bitter poisoned water.
Only tasteless gruel can pass my constricted throat.

Despair plants deadly nightshade in the garden.
Black flowers open at midnight.
Their nectar supplies mind-altering venom
bottled in brown glass with a label that whispers,
"Take me."

Terror presses a circular sander
between my shoulders.
The electric motor's chill whine
cuts through my skull
and freezes reason,
while the 100 grit sandpaper
rips away the delicate skin protecting my spine.

Hatred litters the walk with hard glass.
Seemingly solid, it shatters when gripped by rage.
The shards slice deep
leaving wounds that take moments to bleed
and years to heal.

Conceit argues with the landlord.
"This place is a dump!
Why don't you expand the garden
or add another story?"

I've sent numerous complaints.
The landlord refuses to evict the other tenants,
even though they pay no rent.
I spend weekends driving the neighborhood
in search of a gated community with a "For Rent" sign.

I found one once,
stood outside with my hands on the bars,
looked in, and planned to take a second job,
so I could afford the lease.
I wrote down the phone number
and turned to walk away.
Something caught my eye.
Shards of broken glass on the walkway
glittered like jewels in the summer sun.

How to Build a Weapon of Mass Destruction

You'll need a critical mass of hatred.
Diffuse the powerless through miles of injustice.
Only those enriched with rage will reach the final baffles.
If you're in a hurry, look for weapons-grade material
in the fission products left after societal meltdown.

Machine the dense metal of resentment
into two identical hemispheres.
Label one "Us" and the other "Them,"
Inch them closer,
until both are too hot to touch.
Surround with explosive rhetoric.

To detonate
any spark will do

Rifle Incantation

This rifle's name is Justice.
His slap is a bear's paw
that shatters distant stars.
When he speaks, he splits the sky,
trees topple, and the god of thunder
looks down from heaven.
His barrel is rock, fire,
and shaman's spells. His stock
is soil, sun, and rain.
Like his father and grandfather,
he spits fire at tyrants.

When evil comes,
his stock marries my shoulder.
Like a fine horse,
he senses my wishes
and we move as one.

Justice, do not speak too late
or too soon

Tee Time at Aleppo

To break the siege
select the right driver.
For regional conflicts
a number-three wood works best.
The proper club eliminates
chlorine gas attacks
and most barrel bombs.

Don't leave your golf shoes in the clubhouse
or waste ammunition on Putin.
Erdoğan has it right. Golf carts are essential
when dodging sniper fire.
Be considerate of other players.
Iran, Saudi Arabia, and Kurdistan
are eager to play through.

And if you slice your ball into a minefield,
for God's sake take the penalty stroke
and move on. Save your scorecard.
Your third round is free

Contagion

The mind virus is endemic
spread by cable news anchors
who wipe corporate asses
and then prepare prime-time salads
without washing their hands.

I try to isolate myself
but a woman coughing fundamentalism
knocks on my door, hocks intolerance
on a glossy magazine, and leaves it for me.

Clients wipe noses dripping
with self-defeating economic theories
before shaking my hand
and the IT guy sneezes
partisan slurs on my keyboard.

Even dating is no longer safe
as latex condoms can't completely protect
against traditional gender roles.

So be sure to wear long sleeves after dusk.
The mosquitoes have been listening
to Rush

My Name is Expendable

One nation conceived in peace,
born in liberty, maintained in struggle
until the empire of round hats
turned the summer of love into a winter of hate.
Now street preachers sell poisoned epistemology.
Their new economy
a brick of fake gold that only buys more misery.
The social safety net
devolves into sharpened bamboo stakes.
Riot police of conformity
take tap lessons from the Khmer Rouge. Edward R. Murrow
wins the Pulitzer Prize in he-said, she-said journalism.
David Hume is not amused.

My name is Expendable.
I come bringing cake and questions but
the world doesn't want to hear my song.
Reality's a difficult medium so I loiter
in the mind's apartment experiencing life
through bullet-proof glass:
concrete, boiled frogs, suffering babies in my mailbox,
blood birds, Jane's Eviction, knives wrapped in laughing gas,
and the American public
(that never-ending source of annoyance
and upper respiratory infections).

Existence won't fit in the overhead bin
so pour another glass of powerlessness.
I'll fire up the Crock-Pot of guilt

Before the Anti-Trump Rally

Three hours sleep, one hour early
I wander Balboa Park. If only
today was just about healing crystals
and the gentle girl selling yoga pants.
It's unseasonably hot as if flames of spite
burned the calendar back to August.

There have always been two Americas. Banana Republicans
elected the America of empty promises,
magical thinking, witch hunts, and internment camps;
the America of George Wallace and Bull Connor.

Little hope
for a country this far gone.
If I'm lucky, a lonely exile
of plantains and fried yucca.
The bureaucracy of overseas visas
so disheartening.

There's a Japanese bridge
in the gully below the tea garden.
Up ahead a Baroque tower
and gold-flecked dome of lapis lazuli.
I'll miss this place, its people,
my language

One protester shot in Portland.
My bulletproof vest, too bulky
for today. Ten minutes left. No time
for the Model Train Museum's miniature world,
a world more perfect than this.
I backtrack toward a perilous future

The Parrots of Greenland

The grizzly bear balanced on a unicycle
until Bernie Madoff Elementary let out.
Serves the school board right
for giving AK-47s to kindergarteners.
Everyone knows little hands
can't hold anything bigger than an Uzi

That's how it goes in my Montana beach town.
Kangaroos in wetsuits surf by the pier
and camels in SCUBA gear spear fresh carp.
Our symphony orchestra plays cover tunes
at the Coyote Bar where jellyfish carpaccio
sells for market price. Only arctic rattlesnakes
frown.

Today, the president released his plans to stimulate
the economy with homemade porn.
But you know what they say. It's hard to smell
a gorilla once his breath has been to an orgy.

The Duplicity of Objects

The sun broke its promise
by snorting Oxy
and watching Internet porn
instead of showing up at dawn.
The moon filed for divorce
and took off toward the Oort Cloud
with an unemployed comet.

We pinned our hopes on Jupiter
but all the $25 checks we sent
failed to spark nuclear fusion's match
in its hydrogen core.

Corn, soybeans, and hard northern wheat
walked off the job. Breakfast
hung up a going-out-of-business sign
but don't worry. Lunch will remain open
until the last golden retriever is gone.

Lakes and rivers broke their promise
by sharing dirty needles with lead,
cadmium, and petrochemicals
but don't worry. School water fountains
will stream vodka (while supplies last).

Gravity broke its promise
by selling defense secrets
to finance its gambling habit.
The atmosphere said, "I'm out of here!"
but don't worry. As you hover
gasping for breath, know
that although faithless objects
broke their promises to you
your nerves that carry pain
will keep theirs

Eulogy for the Unfriended

We gather to mourn the loss of
Alice stroking her brown-and-white Saint Bernard,
Barbara embracing her acoustic guitar,
Cheryl who tipsy on Chianti flirted with me
at Don's going-away dinner,
Brad who worked nonviolence into his martial arts
when evicting drunks from a topless bar,
Jeff whose poems meander from sarcasm to irony and back,
Jerry the pot-smoking Vietnam vet always quick with a joke,
and Rob who volleyed batshit ideas with me on the improv
stage.

Holding cognitive dissonance
in respect for nonconforming facts,
I've paused over the unfriend button for years but
what do I say to Harriet who wants me booted
out of the country for not praying to her god?

Scratch a profile picture. Get a noxious gas
of racist dog whistles and totalitarian sympathies –
praise for Joseph McCarthy's blacklist, beating protestors,
and banning the press from exposing politicians' deceit.

Skepticism turns on science and medicine
while leaving hype and spin unquestioned.
Deadly lies infiltrate like a puppy
with a suicide bomb. Measles and whooping cough
back in style. Bound feet, lead makeup, whalebone corsets.

Friendship wears a warning sign.
Trust, an electric fence

City of Acute Angles

I awake in the round hours of night
from dreams of rectangles
and the A-frame I occupied on Euclid Street
with its weeks of rented VHS tapes
and drawer packed elbow deep
with kibble for Spindly the cocker spaniel
who ears flying dived in and out
of neighbors' hedges.

First light scours dreams of home
from shadowy corners and I'm alone again
in one of the high rises tessellated
over the landscape of concrete and rust.
The coffee maker sighs and AC gasps
as picture windows convert solar radiation
to sweat. Since my stove applied for Medicare,
it's become less motivated to fry.
I count the wallpaper's liver spots
while the elevator with sore knees
climbs to my floor. It complains all the way
to the garage and my daily demolition derby.

Roads of concrete, roads of tar,
winding roads, fractal varicose vein roads,
roads to take you away, roads for your return,
roads over bridges, roads with five-way stops,
overpasses, underpasses, cloverleaves,
roads packed with semis, sedans, school busses,
SUVs, pickups, garbage trucks, vans,
and all the occupants' hopes and fears:
figure skates and college funds,
utility bills and mortgage rates,
cheating husbands, shrewish wives,
one class left for that MBA.
I wouldn't trade an AMC Gremlin
with a busted stereo for any of it.

After a day at my office cube, I pedal
the elliptical while pols spout hyperbole on the radio
With movies and novels banished to assisted living
for repeating themselves, I've nothing but a question.
Is this all there is?

Discards

Despite the printed notice
they crowd the dumpster

No room
for turkey bones
and torn wrapping paper

Only a tangle
of dried
      brittle
           branches

These forsaken veterans
shedding brown needles
still smelling
of Christmas

Second Chances

I used to see them all the time
at school, downtown,
and even at my father's office.
They lived in a split-level, Tudor house
a big, sloppy, imperfect family
much like yours or mine.

The oldest, Mercy, got busted for pot but
he saved my ass from that psycho Rick Frost.
Even though everyone whispered
about Charity's mysterious trip to New York
and the rumors that Jeff Stuart got her in trouble,
she made honor roll the following year.
Lots of parents wouldn't let their kids play with Tolerance
because he got caught swiping an F-104 Starfighter model
from Myer's Drugs. For some reason my mom didn't care.

Tolerance's dad had a green VW Karmann Ghia
and hung a tennis ball from a string in the garage
so he knew where to stop. On weekends
he practiced sax with a jazz band. We didn't listen.
Tolerance and I preferred to play Man from U.N.C.L.E.
with the dark glasses and plastic machine gun
I stashed in my father's old briefcase.

I often stayed for dinner
usually macaroni in tomato sauce
served with iceberg lettuce
and the same old joke.
"Look what your father did!"
Then Tolerance's mom would show us the glass eye
in the bottom of her drink.
After I got my license and a girlfriend
I forgot about Second Chances for a while.
One summer I realized they were gone.
Some said they moved to Canada or Norway.
I looked up their relatives, the Fighting Chances,
and drove across town to learn what happened.
They were gone too.

Alcoholic Breakfast

Secrets
between the pancakes, recriminations
in the coffee. She pours suspicion
in a juice glass. He spreads excuses
on the toast, passes the butter dish of abuse.

Eggs stare in awkward silence.
Heaping home fries of denial

Doldrums

Minutes bang together like railroad cars.
I chew Thursday's bread while world leaders
make statements with dead soldiers,
the unprovoked attack merely karma
acting backward in time.

It's always the same.
Bathroom philosophers jumping from bridges
into alcoholics, the cracks in the sidewalk
unrepentant. I hate it
when a paycheck comes
with a death sentence.

Life is God's joke on man.
I'm not laughing.

Theater of Space and Time

You appear on a stage of stopwatches and meter sticks only to have a drink thrown in your face.

"Tracy! How could you?" A woman in a blue skirt drops her glass, buries her face in her hands, and sobs.

"Harriet, I..." You wipe the stinging liquid from your eyes and realize you don't know your lines. How you got here and what led to the woman's outburst remain mysteries. How do you know her name? You stall for time watching all the while for some clue.

"This is the last time you'll make a fool out of me!" Harriet removes a nickel-plated pistol from her purse and aims it at your face.

The nine-millimeter automatic is small enough to fit her tiny hand, but its barrel looms cavernous with doom. Is there some kind of script to follow or should you adlib? You turn to where the prompter should be seated, but your senses can no more pierce the realm beyond this stage of space and time than the twinkle of a firefly on an August night can penetrate the methane clouds that cloak Saturn's moons in permanent darkness. The playwright, director, theater owner, audience, entrances, and exits remain unknown. Only your death imminent or remote is certain.

Future World

Few patrons come to the theme park anymore. Those who do snicker at Kim's spandex bodysuit and aluminum miniskirt. Oh sure, the jetpack and radio-controlled dog still captivate the little boys, but even they rush out of the geodesic dome when they hear the Geiger counter ticking by the nuclear locomotive. It's not like the glory days. Attendance hit the skids after I totaledthe flying car. You can still see the dent it made on the satellite dish. Good thing Kim was safe in the underground lab at the time.

The Home of Tomorrow's been an embarrassment ever since the robot maid's plutonium battery went dead. You can't replace them anymore without a truckload of paperwork. Makes me hot under my Nehru collar. Kim won't clean. Says she's too busy with law school, and I spend most of my time chasing donations to reopen the Pan Am moon base. Is it any wonder that the last tour group found spider webs between the spherical chair and the videophone?

Sometimes I think I should let Taco Bell buy me out and spend the rest of my life playing miniature golf, but it's hard to abandon my dream. Oh well, I've got to teach the Univac his language lesson and pull the control rods out of the reactor to heat up the energy bars. Kim hates it when dinner's late.

Trigger Warning

The following poem contains the phrase "rubber testicles." If the phrase "rubber testicles" upsets you or you simply don't want to hear the phrase "rubber testicles,"please don't listen to this poem.

On the plus side, this poem does not contain the terms *meat curtain, concrete vulva, tungsten-carbide dildo, titanium frenulum, or plutonium clitoris*. If the terms *meat curtain, concrete vulva, tungsten-carbide dildo, titanium frenulum, or plutonium clitoris* offend you or if you simply don't want to hear the terms *meat curtain, concrete vulva, tungsten-carbide dildo, titanium frenulum, or plutonium clitoris;* rest assured they do not appear in the following poem.

The following poem likewise does not include the phrases *pearl necklace, tea bagging, rusty trombone, munching the carpet, choking the gopher, spanking the monkey, or slurping the gherkin*. If the phrases *pearl necklace, tea bagging, rusty trombone, munching the carpet, choking the gopher, spanking the monkey,* or *slurping the gherkin* offend or upset you or if you simply don't want to hear the phrases *pearl necklace, tea bagging, rusty trombone, munching the carpet, choking the gopher, spanking the monkey, or slurping the gherkin,* you're in luck because the *phrases pearl necklace, tea bagging, rusty trombone, munching the carpet, choking the gopher, spanking the monkey, or slurping the gherkin* do not appear in the following poem.

In conclusion the terms *meat curtain, concrete vulva, tungstencarbide dildo, titanium frenulum, plutonium clitoris, pearl necklace, tea bagging, rusty trombone, munching the carpet, choking the gopher, spanking the monkey, or slurping the gherkin* do not appear in the following poem so rest assured you can enjoy this poem without having to hear the terms *meat curtain, concrete vulva, tungsten-carbide dildo, titanium frenulum, plutonium clitoris, pearl necklace, tea bagging, rusty trombone, munching the carpet, choking*

the gopher, spanking the monkey, or slurping the gherkin.
However, the term "rubber testicles" does appear in the following poem. If the term "rubber testicles" upsets you, or you don't want to hear the term "rubber testicles", do not listen to the following poem because the last thing I want to do is expose you to the term "rubber testicles" if you do not want to hear it.

At the Second Coming

parking was atrocious!
After an hour behind a pickup truck
with rubber testicles swinging from its bumper
the only openings I found
were gaps next to a BMW
taking up two spaces.

The ticket line a straightjacket
of sweating bodies - not only Christians
but Buddhists and Hindus too
all shouting into cell phones,
coughing on the back of my neck,
and drowning my sinuses
in second-hand smoke.

Security guards in blue latex gloves everywhere
probing attendees with electric wands
and confiscating liquids. Inside
I bought a bottle of water for $10
and climbed to my seat behind Sherpas
who gasped for breath while Jumbotrons
displayed oil rigs and smiling PR hacks.

I sat down
felt a thump, thump, thump of tiny shoes.
"Please tell your child to stop kicking my seat!"
The father in a short-brimmed fedora rolled his eyes.

Peace, eternal life, universal justice –
I didn't stick around. There's nothing
a crowd can't ruin.

Bankster Rap

Financial bungle – Sometimes it makes me blunder
nearly take the nation under.
Financial bungle – Sometimes makes me blunder
nearly take the nation under.

Gangsters' cash everywhere
in the safe and on the stairs.
We launder dirty money 'cause we just don't care.
The folks at HSBC
make narco smuggling easy.
They won't get caught. They got friends in DC.

Chorus:
Don't push me 'cause I'm close to the hedge
fund. I'm trying to make more bread.
Financial bungle – Sometimes makes me blunder
nearly take the nation under

We took the public's money, rejected further rules.
We do what we want, play the voters for fools
We won't pay a fine, won't go to jail.
Me and my bank are too big to fail
so call me a dog, call me a beagle.
I got Phil Gramm to repeal Glass-Steagall.

[Chorus]

We got connections. Regulators beware!
Mind your own business. Stay out of our affairs.
When business is brisk,
we ignore the risk
and Chase profits wholesale
just like did with the London Whale.

[Chorus]

Your mom on retirement, been days since she ate
'cause the crooks at LIBOR rigged the interest rate.
You can't find a job. Wallet's light as neutrinos
'cause we play global markets like giant casinos.
We take the winnings while you pay the loss.
Worship free markets no matter what the cost.

[Chorus]

Collateralized debt obligation!

The Charge for the Purchase You Made

Eight percent, nine percent
Twelve percent higher
Into a mountain of debt
Grows the six hundred
Charged on the purchase you made.
Your credit card balance
Into a mountain of debt
Grows the six hundred.

Was there no principal paid
Toward the purchase you made?
No, 'cause you're someone to screw
With money to plunder
Your payments go for interest and fees.
Though credit card terms mystify
Yours is not to reason why
Yours is but to buy and buy.
Into a mountain of debt
Grows the six hundred.

Merchants to the right of you
Merchants to the left of you
Merchants in front of you
Plied you with white Zinfandel
To set you up for the hard sell.
Into a mountain of debt,
Your credit score shot all to hell,
Grows the six hundred.

You flashed your checkbook bare.
The minimum payment not there.
Of interest changes beware.
Your low APR now revoked
You realize that you are broke.
If only you hadn't
Charged the six hundred.
Bills to the right of you
Bills to the left of you

Bills behind you
Money's been squandered
In chapter eleven you'll dwell
Your credit score shot all to hell.
Into a mountain of debt
Grew the six hundred.

Your bankruptcy will never fade
Because lenders betrayed
Even though you paid and paid
Your bank account plundered
And bright future waylaid.

Halloween in Cambodia

So you sucked the blood
from a girl or two
and think that you're a fright.
Turn into a bat,
drop the hemostat.
You're a creature of the night.

You make your escape
in a black silk cape
and sleep inside a tomb.
Dream 'til noon
of a dining room
and all who you'll consume.

You think there's nothing left to fear
but your fangs won't help you here.
Brace yourself, my dear.
Brace yourself, my dear

for a Halloween in Cambodia
where even vampires scream.
It's a Halloween in Cambodia.
No escaping this bad dream.

Werewolves might take
a sheep or two
and kill them while they flail
but they can't outdo the human race
making death
on industrial scale.

No candy bars
or trick or treat
keep Khmer Rouge away.
Bullets in backs
knives to throats
in gruesome porch displays.

Now the death squad's had their fun.
Even monsters turn and run.
Better flee, my son.
Better flee, my son

from a Halloween in Cambodia
where skulls are stored on racks.
It's a Halloween in Cambodia's
megalomaniac.

Pol Pot Pol Pot Pol Pot Pol Pot
Pol Pot Pol Pot Pol Pot Pol Pot

If you spend Halloween in Cambodia,
you'd better change your plans.
It's a Halloween in Cambodia.
No killer's worse than man.
Pol Pot

Truth Serum

The Pope admitted, "We made the whole Jesus thing up."
On his visit to the Vatican the Dalai Lama said the same
about Buddha. "We sure got a kick out of that one."
The same day my wife confessed,
"Although I find sex with you repulsive,
it sure beats working full time."

It must have been something in the water.
Doctors ridiculed their patients' vaginal itching.
The President called the American public,
"a bunch of whining, self-indulgent morons."

Later, I waited at the curb for a gap
in the torrent of speeding distracted metal,
when a woman, I didn't even know,
brought her green Land Rover to a halt for me to cross.
I found a brown paper bag of my neighbor's
heirloom tomatoes on my doorstep.
It was a good day.

Heaven

My apartment's walls shut the insanity out, everything
except the ocean's moist sigh through the window.
The PBS station has signed off leaving silence behind.
I read in a golden cone of lamplight. Bukowski sings
the joy of solitude. His poems remind me how lucky I am
the corporate empire-builders have passed me by.

Sleep follows its natural cycle.
While others chase morning futility on crowded roads,
I wake to oatmeal and fine green tea. Soon my pen herds
stray thoughts on a white legal pad.

Terry Gross on the radio, a drive to the coffee shop,
Waves glitter like facets of a giant sapphire.
Nose-ring girl behind the counter, the veranda
next to the friendly pine, a hummingbird on its branch.
Numbers inked in my checkbook dwindle,
but I don't worry today.

Late afternoon, the sun paints my walls orange
in the few hours of quiet before neighbors return.

Coexistence with Nature

Chet showed me a picture of a black bear in his driveway.
Unfortunately, it was behind the wheel of an SUV.
Having only a learner's permit, a licensed driver needed
to accompany it but no one volunteered.

Chet's taken this coexistence thing too far.
There are elk in the dishwasher
and opossums in the microwave.
Even when otters yell, "Marco! Polo!" from the pool,
the manatee won't get out of the bath.
Chipmunks play cards into the wee hours
and deer wont' turn the stereo down
despite numerous visits from the cops.

Raccoons drink milk straight from the carton.
Rabbits eat the last of the cereal. The mountain lion
borrows shirts without asking, tossing them
on a moose's antlers when done. Chet's porcupine
has an unhealthy obsession with a hairbrush.

The beaver's orthodontist bills emptied
coyote's college fund and left wolverine
without a rented tux for the senior prom.
Don't get me started about the crows.

Crime Wave

I don't know about murder hornets but cockroaches loiter in
my cupboards and drunk-and-disorderly geese honk to hiphop
music until dawn. But you know what they say. When
Canada sends its waterfowl, they don't send their best. They
send hooligans, delinquents, and scofflaws smuggling maple
syrup and back bacon in their beaks. Law enforcement is
a joke. Cops look the other way when coyotes shoplift beef
jerky from the 7-Eleven. They even let the black bear who
broke into my kitchen off with a warning. Otters or longhorn
beetles must be paying them off. When I discovered a
blue jay was using my credit-card number to buy fifty-pound
sacks of birdseed online, I didn't bother reporting it.

I blame the media. With all the lewdness on those PBS nature
documentaries is it any wonder that gangs of whitetailed
deer shake down business owners and woodchucks
sell crack cocaine by Mrs. Blumtrapster's petunias? Hell, the
only reason the feds locked up that bighorn sheep was for
tax evasion. Thank God, the murder hornets haven't made
it here, yet. The manslaughter spiders and assault-and-battery
weevils are bad enough. Why, just last week, there was a
home invasion of carpenter ants, all with their little saws and
hammers, at the Dundersteads' place. I've taken to keeping
my shotgun loaded and propped by the door. If any mallards,
sparrows, or nuthatches want to mess with me or mine, I'll
be ready.

Dangerous Vegetables

Spiteful as landmines
root vegetables lie in wait.
A carrot can blow off a man's foot
while turnips pack enough C-4
to take out an M1 Abrams tank.

I've known of vegetables' duplicity
ever since mom first served boiled spinach.
Creamed corn races motorcycles
without a helmet while artichokes
wrap piano wire around their stalks
to strangle unsuspecting victims.

Sweet potatoes fling lawn darts
on the playground. Onions
do back flips off the trampoline.
Bell peppers smoke in bed.
Squash leaves a space heater too close
to the curtains. Iceberg lettuce
sinks the Titanic.

Ferment cabbages with a little salt
and they annex the Sudetenland.
Watercress torpedoes merchant ships.
Daikon radishes yell "Banzai!"
only to have their suicide charge
met with habaneros' flamethrowers.
Most insidious of all,
beets shoulder Kalashnikovs
while installing SS-4 missiles in Cuba.

So, when the USDA recommends five servings a day,
you'd better turn that food pyramid upside-down.
Mustard greens, mustard gas
I don't think so.

I Want to be Jean-Paul Sartre

Won't you be my Simone?
We'll watch ghetto kids with thick volumes of Descartes and
Husserl argue the meaning of being on unused basketball courts.
Philosophy fans will pay fortunes for front-row seats to see
the president pitch the first question on opening day.

Office workers will set down newsprint on subway seats
and exclaim, "How about those phenomenologists?
What a dynamite syllogism they pulled off in the fourth quarter!"
Shoppers will troll souvenir stands for black berets,

mass produced in China. Scholars will wade
through mobs of panty-waving groupies. TV viewers
will abandon "Survivor" for a new reality show,
"Authentic." And politicians will propose bond issues
for new libraries to keep
rival cities from luring thinkers away.

I want to be Jean-Paul Sartre.
And if you would be my Simone,
I know a way.

Your gods have abandoned you like a management team
absent on a long junket. Only the shadow play of mind on a screen
of dumb matter occupies the CEO's chair. Will you slave
in your cubicle through dinner, fritter away the afternoon
eating beignets in a Paris café, or collect baguettes for the
poor? The locomotive of responsibility crushes your heart. You
must choose.

No Artillery at the Dinner Table

The look of anticipation
retreats from Junior's face.
Sis sticks out her tongue
squirts him in the eye with mustard gas.
He levels his howitzer.

"What did I tell you kids?"
Father's fork thrusts deep
across the kitchen table
smashes though lines of entrenched potatoes
in a blitz toward the roast.

In a desperate effort to buy time
Mom harasses
his supply lines with oven mitts.
Junior counterattacks
with a Jell-O mold
forming pincers with Sis's
VI Mechanized Infantry Corps.

Father's rapid advance grinds to a halt
but the wily survivor of
the Battle of the Saturday Carwash
is not to be undone. His forces
pivot to the left encircling the Jell-O.
Meanwhile his sappers
set off charges under the sauce boat
flooding the tablecloth with sawmill gravy
to create a diversion.

Father withdraws his fork.
The front stabilizes in an uneasy truce
by the time Mom sets out the pumpkin pie.

"It's so nice to have a family dinner."

Decision Theory

I'm making a spreadsheet
to decide whether to kill my dog.
That big, lumbering pile of fur
is getting older and dammit
it's time to run my household like a business.

I score each of Dusty's features from -5 to +5,
+5 being the best. Gazing up with adoring eyes,
chin on paw, and tail thumping the carpet
earns Dusty a +5 while drinking from the toilet
or knocking over the trash and dragging used Kleenex
into the living room moves him closer to oblivion.

I'm in the middle of a computer simulation
of future vet bills when Joan notices me
in the monitor's blue glow.
She just doesn't get it.
I weighted each of Dusty's traits
according to its importance
to account for what I value.
I'm not inhuman, after all.

Why can't she see
that the rigor of the binomial distribution
and numbers' cool, green rationality
deliver choices free of passion and prejudice?
Besides, she's hosted a sloppier calculation
between her ears for months.

Eyes squinting and neck straining
I input the remaining data so fast
the mouse jitters like a relativistic Chihuahua
at an espresso bar. The miracle of Moore's Law
tallies the weighted sum and the results are
terminal.

Tail wagging and ignorant of the computer's verdict,
Dusty drops a slobbery tennis ball
at my feet and nudges my hand with his nose.
How can a spreadsheet model loyalty
or decency?
You're safe, buddy!

Polar Bears Make Bad Neighbors

especially the one with jailhouse tattoos.
Like, I'm supposed to believe those teardrops
are just for ringed seals! It's always the same
he and his friends partying at midnight,
yelling, "How about another Molson, eh?"
Then he's drunk outside my door
pleading to borrow ice. I pretend I'm asleep
as if anyone could sleep with Avril Lavigne
blaring from his stereo.

He never works. All he does
is sit around the pool in his Speedos.
With all that spare time he should haul
his garbage bags to the dumpster
instead of leaving them on his stoop.

Don't get me started on those delinquents of his.
Mother abandoned them at age two.
Now they smoke cigarettes by the 7 Eleven.
Broke into my kitchen
ate five pounds of frozen burgers.
Cops wouldn't do a thing
even after I showed them
the footprints in the spilled honey
and tooth marks on my adult DVDs.

Endangered Species Act – my ass!

Rich in Antioxidants

Crimson juice
thick as blood
sweet
the earth trembles
     beneath
refrigerated shelves
       splits open
black chariot, black horses
Pluto drags another Birkenstock maiden
     {away}

But now
even more sinister
underground pomegranate orchards
UV lamps   orange extension cords
aqueducts with blind, albino fish
mass production
great barges plying the River Styx
bringing bottles
to a grocery store
near you

Another Day at the Office for Apollo

Just once I'd like to sleep in. I swear, when I retire, I'm moving
to Norway. Buy a little place north of the Arctic Circle
and spend six months in glorious darkness. Not that that's
going to happen any time soon, especially after Zeus replaced
our pensions with 401 (k)s. Have you been watching the
market? Olive futures tanked and the drachma's in the toilet.

I can never get a decent cup of coffee up here. Zoning board
wouldn't let them put in a Dunkin Donuts. Said its décor
would clash with the unique character of Mt. Olympus. Really
gripes my ass.

Don't get me started on insurance companies. After my son
banged up the chariot on his little joy ride, they wouldn't let
me take it to the dealer. No! Sent it to some chop shop run by
Scythians. Scythians! Now it's supposed to be my fault Helios
can't stay in its orbit. Don't blame global warming on me!

And health insurance! Damn pissants told me sunburn is a
preexisting condition. It's not like I'm going to die. I'm immortal
for Zeus's sake!

What drives me nuts is taxes. I worked hard for everything I
got and the government is giving my money away to a bunch
of freeloading Dionysians. The middle class built this mythology
and all they're doing is giving us the shaft. Take it
from me. The whole cosmology is going down the tubes.

Gentle World

An inventor modified AR-15s to accept
PEZ dispensers in their magazine feeds.
Fighters traded boxing gloves
for teddy bears; doctors
discovered chocolate and espresso
worked better than surgery; and Cuddle Ryu,
a new martial art, swept the nation.

Cops traded pistols for squirt guns
loaded with craft beer and disarmed
suspects with the phrase,
"You look like you need a hug."
States converted prisons to animal shelters
burying inmates in squirming puppies.

The military joined in. Cruisers
bombarded shores with blueberry muffins.
The Air Force dyed its uniforms purple
and repurposed Minuteman II missiles
to deliver pizza in thirty minutes or less.

Russia responded
with SS-19s loaded with kasha and pirozhki.
Not to be outdone, North Korea sent bottles
of fiery soju marching across the DMZ
after exploding its largest rice-and-kimchi bomb yet.

Smallpox and Ebola mutated
so the worst sufferers could expect
was a mild, paisley rash.
Hurricanes apologized, dropping granola bars
and bottled water in their paths.
The San Andreas Fault
worked off its aggression
by swaying to the Grateful Dead.

Somewhere
in a fiction writer's mind
swarthy terrorists kidnapped
the President's daughter
and forced her to pole dance
on a burning American flag.

Noting the remote control's power button
existed for just such an emergency
a top CIA analyst acted.
Outrage collapse
to a glowing, white dot
on the TV screen

Tenderness

As a reward for their loyalty, the Corn Maiden
turned our pets into people. We welcomed them, at first,
but without fur and floppy ears their antics aren't cute any-
more. A hamster wheel, the size of a B-52 Stratofortress,
wakes the neighborhood at 2 AM. Ahanu digs up rhododen-
drons to bury his 401k statements and puppy eyes don't go
far after humping the instructor's leg in the sexual harass-
ment seminar. Tsídii's mistaken attempts to hatch them pre-
vent the Russells from keeping eggs in the house. Mósí leaves
dead deer and the occasional bear cub on the porch.

We petitioned the Corn Maiden
to change our friends back.
"Have patience," she said,
"They haven't had much practice
being human."

Ode to Stir-Fried Tofu and Broccoli

Golden cubes and bright green vegetable welcome me
whether I'm soaked in Shanghai, frazzled in Manassas,
or in the only Chinese restaurant in Somewhere Montana.

Soothing as a warm bath.
Comforting as a mother's embrace.

My back against the booth's fake leather
I serve myself American style,
pile rice on my plate, spoon stir fry on top
while recorded Chinese strings serenade.

Black bean sauce clings to rough skin
of fried tofu, lodges between green florets.
Scallions and Shitake mushrooms
play keep-away from plastic chopsticks.

Satisfying nutritious   No animal gave
its life for this meal. I refill
the small, white cup
with jasmine tea
until the stainless-steel pot
is empty.

No matter what
the fortune cookie says
I am a lucky man.

A Taco Truck on Every Corner

My culture is a very dominant culture, and it's imposing
and it's causing problems. If you don't do something about
it, you're going to have taco trucks on every corner.
Marco Gutierrez, Latinos for Trump

Taste the America that still can be
where brown hands and smiling faces
save your late-start morning
with flour tortillas dripping in butter.
Flavors and syllables roll off the tongue: *chorizo, adobo,*
pico de gallo, carne asada, al pastor, huevos rancheros,
chile relleno.

Not on every block but maybe every square mile
a Korean fusion truck with its K taco:
bulgogi beef, kimchi, and sweet fiery gochujang.

Diversity sets the best table:
pillowy Ethiopian injera, Vietnamese banh mi
melding Asian and European flavors on French bread,
Pad Thai, chicken and waffles, the Cuban sandwich,
gyros, baba ghanoush, shawarma, sushi, tempura,
samosas, lumpia, biryani, General Tso's chicken.
Did I forget Italy? Who can imagine lives
without pizza, lasagna, and Chianti?

America,
your banquet awaits!

Do I Have Time to Read One More?

NO! Mastodons still roamed the Earth when tonight's poetry reading began but you wouldn't know that, would you? You arrived ten minutes ago and cut in front of the fifteen readers who are still waiting. Two passed into menopause and one developed an enlarged prostate during the feature. You told the MC you had to run off to your daughter's wedding which will happen next to your grandfather's simultaneous funeral across from the baseball field hosting your son's little league playoff. If you're in such a rush, how did you find the time to read us seven poems, your head down staring at your papers so you didn't see the next reader on the open mic list die from old age. Honestly it feels more like you read seventeen due to your long-winded introductions. No one cares about how the rhubarb marmalade you spread on your gluten-free toast inspired your poem. Each member has shown you more patience than that of the love child who would have resulted if Gandhi, Martin Luther King, and Mother Teresa had had a three-way. For God's sake, have some consideration! Some of us would like to visit our grandchildren before they become parents, like to walk among the pines before the sun swells to a ball of radioactive flame that engulfs the Earth.

Jon Wesick is a regional editor of the San Diego Poetry Annual. He's published hundreds of poems and stories in journals such as the *Atlanta Review, Berkeley Fiction Review, Metal Scratches, Pearl, Slipstream, Space and Time, Tales of the Talisman,* and *Zahir*. The editors of *Knot Magazine* nominated his story "The Visitor" for a Pushcart Prize. His poem "Meditation Instruction" won the Editor's Choice Award in the 2016 Spirit First Contest. Another poem "Bread and Circuses" won second place in the 2007 African American Writers and Artists Contest. "Richard Feynman's Commute" shared third place in the 2017 Rhysling Award's short poem category. Jon is the author of the poetry collection *Words of Power, Dances of Freedom* as well as several novels and most recently *The Prague Deception*.

http://jonwesick.com

Jon Wesick's poems brim with absurdist encounters and irreverent meditations. With themes ranging from Zen to politics, they star polar bear neighbors, muse on the nature of the Buddha, bemoan the lack of parking at the Second Coming. Wesick plays with language like an accomplished juggler and uses his unexpected imagery and his sense of humor for a biting societal critique. An entertaining and thought-provoking collection.

Agnes Vojta, author of A Coracle for Dreams

Jon Wesick knows all the words. I know this is true because most of them appear in his book The Shaman in the Library. At least the good ones, the ones you didn't expect to hear and too often forget to use yourself. They're in there and they keep coming like an elusive never-ending quantum energy source that only he has the understanding to operate. These words create a world you may want to avoid actually existing in, but you sure want to find out what happens. When I'm making a spreadsheet to decide whether to kill my dog comes along, for example, it's biologically impossible to not keep reading to see where this is going. Even words you may not want to read are in there which he, thankfully acknowledges in a litany of trigger warning phrases that give you the opportunity to choose for yourself. Sometimes you get the illusion everything is fine, but then suddenly larvae and banshees and polar bears with jailhouse tattoos come along and you're reminded these are poems forged from an electrified imagination. The Buddha pops in to ground you, and, of course, there's food at the end because you can't make your way through such an epic collection without a little nosh at the end. One thing I know for sure: You should read this book. You should let Jon Wesick redefine poetry for you (at least 25 times!) You may be grateful to return to your own world, but you'll be sneaking glimpses back into his over and over. And yes, Jon, you do have time to read one more poem. Please do.

Rick Lupert, author of The Tokyo-Van Nuys Express